THE

Pattern

The Lord's Prayer

THE

Pattern

The Lord's Prayer

ARCHIE MURRAY

PRAYING BELIEVERS SERIES

THE PATTERN
Copyright © 2025 by Archie Murray

ISBN: 978-1-4866-2215-3
eBook ISBN: 978-1-4866-2216-0

Word Alive Press
119 De Baets Street Winnipeg, MB R2J 3R9
www.wordalivepress.ca

WORD ALIVE
—P R E S S—

Cataloguing in Publication information can be obtained from Library and Archives Canada.

DEDICATION

This second book on prayer is written for the many wonderful people I have prayed with in my life. Many of them, myself included, stumbled and mumbled and fumbled through prayer meetings. We wanted to express ourselves to the Lord in prayer. Many people taught us by example, but in my entire life as a believer, nobody ever suggested I look at the Lord's Prayer for guidance, strange as this may seem. I have confirmed this over the last decade by asking people if they ever seriously looked at the Lord's Prayer to find out how to pray. Not one person said that they did. Of course, others may have.

For many, this passage of the Sermon on the Mount has been spoiled by the persistent practice of vain repetition in churches and schools where it's recited with a religious sobriety and depth but totally disconnected from reality. A magical moment is imagined, but a pleasant, religious feeling is all that it returns. It's forgotten quicker than it takes to recite the few words contained therein. For the believer, this is a great loss.

I dedicate this book to all those who want Jesus to teach them to pray. I pray that they might be liberated from human, needs-based misery and into the real power of uplifting, biblical, Christ-honouring, godly prayer as taught by the Lord Jesus.

My hope in writing this trilogy is to encourager a deeper look at Jesus's pattern for prayer. I believe with all my heart that it could transform the prayer meetings of countless believers and churches—*if* and only *if* we can understand it apart from any religious spirit and simply as a real and profound pattern, guide, structure, and platform. It's certainly an inspiration and teaching on prayer. Our private and corporate prayer needs renovation!

Contents

Acknowledgements

Many books have been written on prayer. Many of them I have read. While these three books are all my own thoughts and considerations, I realize that in a lifetime, all of us have been influenced by people better than ourselves. I want to acknowledge all those ancient and a few modern writers who influenced me in my youth, in particular from the annals of the history of the great Reformation churches and the earlier period of good men in God's Church. My direct experience is from the modern Evangelical Baptist and Reformed Baptist movements. If any good results from these books, I heartily acknowledge that the best came from them over years of influence. The poorer content is undeniably entirely mine.

PREFACE

I approach the subject of the Lord's Prayer with great caution. Without exaggeration, I've been afraid to write on it for years. For me, it's a holy and high subject of utmost, even terrible, import. Prayer defines us. The Bible teaches that both private and corporate prayer is a moment when sinners commune with God! We call Him Father, and we realize that He's in heaven. We declare Him hallowed (set apart). We cry out that His Kingdom comes and His will be done on earth as in heaven. In the midst of this, we ask for simple bread and humbly ask for forgiveness, which we often refuse to give. Throughout the pattern, but specifically at the end, we resist evil.

The passage in the Sermon on the Mount is, in my opinion, the greatest comment on prayer the Christian Church possesses. The Lord Jesus Himself is the giver of this pattern for prayer. My meagre self shrinks from approaching it, lest I pollute it in my attempt to exalt it.

Chapter 1
LONELINESS IN PRAYER

"When you pray, say: Our ... " (Luke 11:2).

The picture created by the earlier passages is of a solitary individual in a secret place. The pattern is all in plural language. What are we to make of this? On the one hand, it is Jesus addressing a group of people and simply using language set by that context. It's also Jesus specifically addressing each individual in the group, thereby indicating possible encouragement for that individual. When he is praying, he is solitary yet not alone.

Prayer for the believer can be a lonely place. This part of the Sermon on the Mount is about being discrete, even secret, in our good works. Personal prayer should be likewise. Don't declare it; don't do it to be seen. Indeed, hide it! It's your unique time with the Lord, just for you and Him. It can be lonely, until faith sees clearly.

The Lord calls us to pray often. This call lands weightless, like a dove on a branch, a soft pressure on the sensitive heart. It tells us that the time for prayer has come. Sometimes it's the diligent habit of daily pray. For some, it's a heavy desperation. The pattern intends that this will be a precious experience for the believer, the birthright of every believer. God wants to fellowship with us, so He invites us to speak with Him!

Perhaps more amazingly, He intends to listen to us. Nothing is too big, too small, too short, or too long. He is waiting. He is never too busy. He is serious. He intends to make this time of fellowship count, so He warmly invites us to come away to a private room to pray. He isn't looking for a practised performance. He's looking for a real person—the real you. The pattern of the Lord's Prayer will only accept you with both heart and mind as you genuinely use your own thoughts and words with all your heart, however unpoetic.

When believers approach prayer with this pattern for the first time, they're often reduced to silence. The cold fact is that the pattern is not about me. Concepts we assume are essential are absent at the beginning, such as confession of failings and sin, and sharing of problems. For many, these are the essence of praying, but they're left to near the end!

Isolation pushes us into ourselves, whether it's physical, psychological, or spiritual. It can be a lonely, painful place. Often it's a hurtful experience that marginalized us and drove us to pray. Yet this isolated place can be where deep dealings between ourselves and God occur. Any one of these three types of isolation is sufficient to bring us to our knees. The Lord will use all three if He finds us stubborn.

In the place of prayer, we must be totally independent in spirit before God. No other voice should be heard. Everything about the context Jesus gives is designed to make this a unique, private, and personal moment between me and God. There can be a temptation to shrink from the isolation and a reluctance to go to the private place of prayer. But Jesus counsels us to say "Our!"

God's call to pray, my desire to pray, and even the call of my needs often come to me in the midst of my happiest moments, especially legitimate family joys—times when I did not want to be alone. Frequently, that was when I had to pray. I learned to be sensitive to this call and overcome my reluctance. Perhaps you can relate to this sense of solitariness in your own experience. Of course, if you're a young, busy mother, the solitary moment might be just what you need! That's fine.

Then I studied the Lord's Prayer in some depth for a preaching engagement. The apparent conflict between these two words came to my attention: When "you" pray, say "our." Jesus was teaching the disciples to pray as individuals. They weren't asking how to have a corporate prayer meeting. They wanted to be able to pray by themselves, individually. The lesson was about private prayer.

Jesus tells individuals, alone in a secluded place, to say "our." Why not "my" Father, or simply "Father"? The question we need to ask is: "If we're not alone, who and where are all the others?"

To an observer of me in my room alone, I am a picture of all that solitude suggests, good and bad. But faith transforms everything for the believer. Of course God is here when I pray. This is warm sunshine bursting through the window of my cabin on a cool spring morning. We are alone when we pray. But "our" indicates company!

This "our" could point to the fact that Jesus, the speaker, is also there as we approach the throne of God. His presence makes us welcome there. That turns solitary me into Jesus and me. I can't pray without Him. I can't actually ever pray in isolation. The scriptures also tell us that "*the Spirit himself intercedes for us*" (Romans 8:26, ESV). Are there other people there? Yes, there are.

All over this world, other isolated saints are praying. Along with you and me, they've found a private place to pray and are, by faith, also around the throne of God. In spiritual reality, a great multitude surrounds the throne of God with us. Countless saints, all gathered, all praying. Some weren't even as blessed as me in my tiny cupboard. Russian believers and Chinese believers at that time were in Communist prisons in both countries. They didn't see their friends or family for years.

At the time I first thought about this, I was in peaceful, happy Scotland in comfort and safety. My family and friends were accessible to me anytime, just not right now. This realization came to me quite powerfully and changed me profoundly in terms of my understanding of loneliness in prayer and its purpose.

In a sense, the great cloud of witnesses in Hebrews is there, at the Throne of Grace. When we pray, we're not alone because we're surrounded by saints and angels. God the Father, God the Son, and God the Holy Spirit, the three in one, are all there. Prayer has never been lonely since.

I'm not praying to saints—they'd be appalled if I did. The same cloud that shrouded the three disciples on the Mount of

Transfiguration, where they took equal notice of Moses and Abraham, would overshadow me and chill my heart, calling me back to see "*Jesus only*" (Matthew 17:8).

I have found this thought to be a great joy. When I pray, I thank God for all those around His throne. My secret place is not a secret in heaven. I am not alone when I approach the throne of God in prayer. An old hymn says …

> Around the throne God in Heaven,
> Thousands of children stand,
> Children whose sins are all forgiven,
> A holy, happy band.
> Singing, "Glory, glory,
> Glory be to God on high.[1]

Next time you hear the call to pray, go to your secret place. When you're alone, pray "*Our* Father," and by faith hear a glorious "AMEN!" Thus encouraged, pray joyfully with all your heart and might to our Father.

Jesus begins His guidance on prayer by turning our inward gaze outwards. Faith sees a warmer picture of private prayer than does unbelief. It's not a miserable, monastic confinement. We must often refresh our view of prayer. Make sure your feelings are made to follow faith, fixed on God's Word.

---

[1] Anne H. Shepherd, "Around the Throne of God in Heaven," HymnTime, accessed July 12, 2024, http://www.hymntime.com/tch/htm/a/r/o/t/arotgodh.htm.

Notes

_____

_____

_____

_____

_____

Chapter 2
INTRODUCING GOD

"... Our Father ... " (Matthew 6:9).

At the very beginning of the pattern, Jesus reminds us to consider who God is—He is our Father. People who don't know their father often float through the world like lost souls. People who know who he is but have no relationship with him lack an anchor and guide. We must know to whom we're praying. Jesus identifies God by using the title "Father." We must understand how that affects our prayers.

God is our Father. He formed us out of nothing and gave us life! The word "Father" conveys concepts like generation, relationship, provision, authority, protection, as well as a substantial sense of belonging for us, and a fundamental sense of ownership for God. This should enthuse us with a certain character—a reflected character. We need to know who our Father is in order to understand who we are. We are His children. Consider how that makes you think and feel as you come to pray.

In prayer, we grow in our knowledge of God. We experience Him and get to know Him personally. Knowledge of God's Fatherhood isn't about learning a doctrinal statement, though this helps. The real issue is getting to know Him and developing a real relationship. The relationship with a human father may have been missed for any number of reasons, but we can experience all that fatherly love and much more when we pray. So say "Our Father." The introductory two words tell us that we have a divine Father and siblings. Saying "Our Father" is now comfortable and comforting.

Declaring God as our Father when we pray instantly removes the attention from ourselves and directs it to God. Make it fresh every time you pray. In this respect, prayer is a "family" matter.

What we're looking at here is the introductory content of our prayer. With the opening words of the pattern, Jesus challenges our thinking about prayer. The words are intended to bring concepts to our mind as we begin to pray. Prayer inspires thoughtfulness and inquisitiveness and encourages learning and experience. Prayer introduces God to His children. He knows us and has known us in the past. We may not have known the Lord until later in life, but we still have a lifetime left to get to know Him as "our Father" in prayer.

Chapter 3
THE CHILDREN OF GOD

God wants us to approach Him as our Father. He also wants us to see ourselves as His children. Lacking this sense of identity causes us to act like worthless beggars, both in His presence and in the world. No father wants his children to feel less than they are. It's a bad reflection on a father if his children can't identify with him properly. Afraid, lacking respect, disobedient, arrogant, needy, desperate, helpless, incompetent children, untaught and messed up—this is a bad reflection on any father, and neither is it a true reflection of who we are as the children of God!

This paternal element in prayer produces a confident believer who, having just been in conversation with God, is afraid of no one! This child of God is at peace with himself and the world of circumstances, simply because he knows his Father. He carries himself with a deep-seated strength based upon this relationship. The children of God are profoundly but humbly confident. They need no arrogance because they have a constant sense of belonging to God. They're afraid of nothing. The child of God has a dignity that reflects who they are.

We are the children of God. When we come to prayer, we must learn how to handle this relationship, to take strength from who He is and who we are. Prayer is where we begin to develop this practice. Jesus wants us to take hold of this reality. We are praying to Almighty God—who is our Father!

Chapter 4
ENGAGED BUT NOT ENTANGLED

"… in heaven …" (Matthew 6:9).

Jesus turns our attention to where God is. He is *"in heaven."* Having just comforted us, reminding us that we're not alone, He takes "our Father" and places Him firmly out of our reach in heaven! How does this awareness of distance, in terms of location, help us when we pray? There's a rigidity about the phrase that jars, yet there's a picturesque benefit for us in the fact that God is in heaven.

Consider the fact that when we're trying to help someone, it's often beneficial to be outside the theatre of trouble. We aren't part of the problem. God is never part of the problem.

Archimedes said: "Give me a place to stand on, and I can move the earth."[2]

Our Father in heaven. Engaged but not entangled. The lesson from this part of the Lord's Prayer is that God has a place where He is. From there He rules the world and all that is in it. This world is not His home. Heaven is not threatened by this world. God

---

[2] T.L. Heath (Ed.), *The Works of Archimedes with the Method of Archimedes* (New York, NY: Dover Publications, Inc., 1953), xix.

is not moved by anything that happens here in terms of human trouble. He's most certainly interested in us. The evidence for this is that "… *God so loved the world that He gave His only begotten Son, that whoever believes in Him should not perish but have everlasting life*" (John 3:16).

God's intention is not to fix the world but to take His children out of this world to be where He is—in heaven. It won't be until the mid-point in the pattern that we deal with the time between now and heaven. Initially in prayer Jesus takes us to heaven by faith. We pray in an isolated room in this world, but faith raises the praying believer to heaven.

God sees everything from heaven. Think about how much time you spend explaining your circumstances to the Lord, as though He doesn't know what's happened to you. He sees everything while not being subsumed by anything. We think we see things clearly. We imagine that we understand the whole problem. But we don't have a heavenly view of things. If we did, we might not be so worried about them. This reference to God in heaven can comfort us. As we pray according to the pattern, faith lifts us to where our Father is. As we follow the pattern, we also begin to see this world from a heavenly perspective— that is, from God's perspective. The theological explanations are much more thorough, but for a simple meditation, this is sufficient to give us a little insight into the benefit of "*Our Father* (being) *in heaven.*"

As you enter the presence of God to pray, these initial words and concepts condition us in God's presence before we ask for anything for ourselves! Note also that your prayer, so framed, will reach our Father in heaven.

Surely the believer who follows this pattern in prayer is well prepared to commune with God. Their hearts are engaged, their minds are in tune, and they have prepared themselves for an important meeting. They may have laid aside their own special interests. There is nothing rushed or sloppy, nothing ordinary. This type of praying is a productive spiritual exercise of believing prayer.

Notes

_____

_____

_____

_____

_____

Chapter 5
IT'S ALL ABOUT GOD

Heaven isn't disturbed at all by praying believers. They don't bring the clutter and noise of the world with them. Their praying is only about our Father in heaven. They actually fit very well into heaven because their focus, like heaven, is totally on God Himself. God the Father fills all they think and say. The woes of the world haven't been laid out or expressed yet. In fact, they have been laid aside! You might not think this is possible yet, but Jesus encourages us to do just that—lay aside all the burdens and care. Speak only of your heavenly Father.

Jesus brings us to a contented place. The pattern brings us to a quieter place—not unravelled by needs or invaded by trouble. Jesus presents a peaceful picture of solitary, believing prayer. So far, prayer is time spent in the presence of God, who is secure, at rest, and in control of everyone and everything, everywhere.

When you pray, say "*Our Father in heaven.*" We're told to "say" this. While prayer isn't to be reduced to mere recitation, it is nevertheless a vocal exercise, sometimes before it becomes a heart exercise. The spoken word carries the speaker. The silent

The silent word is carried by the speaker. The spoken word carries the speaker.

word is carried by the speaker. Silent prayers are okay, but spoken prayer is better for the one praying! It's not a rule, but it is the advice of Jesus, especially when we begin to pray.

We always want to rush on! But before we do, let's ask: What is it about this heaven that meets me upon entry into my tiny chamber? Surely some understanding might fill my little room with the presence of God. God in heaven is a picture of a perfect place, filled with peace, contentment, holiness, and God-centred worship. It's worship with no mention of this world's cares. No physical ailments! No one is dying! No sadness or tears in heaven. That's the environment in which God hears our prayers. So don't jar heaven by carrying bundles and bags filled with the woes of a fallen world into the throne room of God. We need to hear heaven singing, heaven worshipping, heaven happy as we begin to pray! Let your praying be scented with wonder. Let heaven invade your private place. Let heaven into your heart before you say anything about this world or yourself! That's a good start to a day.

We must not pollute heaven. Heaven must purify us.

Chapter 6
What They Do in Heaven

"… Hallowed … " (Matthew 6:9).

Prayer is the hallowing of God's name! It's not merely saying the phrase! Hallowing God's name is what they do in heaven—this is real prayer. The things we do, and everything that happens, hallows God's name. It brings glory to Him. Those in heaven hallow God's name in that all they say and do brings adoration to God. Everything in heaven turns their eyes upon Him. He is our Father in heaven.

"Hallowed" means "set-apart." We are to declare God's name as set apart, as special in and of itself. His name is incomparable and above all others. This worship will remind us of God's greatness, His awesome holiness and majestic righteousness. "God the Father" is the name by which we are to initially approach Him in prayer, according to Jesus's pattern.

Prayer is not initially about reminding God of who we are—needy sinners. Prayer is about reminding us of who God is—our Father. This introductory expression will set us in a good place.

Prayer is not about reminding God of who we are. It's about reminding us of who God is.

"*You shall not take the name of the Lord your God in vain, for the Lord will not hold him guiltless who takes His name in vain*" (Exodus 20:7). "In vain" means "carelessly." We must not rush over this name! Hallowing God's name must be a true reflection of our heart. By this pattern, in this room in secret, an attitude can be established that will have resounding consequences in the private and public life of the individual and the Church in the world. We will become a people who revere God in a full and balanced, serious lifestyle. The evidence is a people who feel deeply hurt at the misuse of His holy name.

Let the psalmist David teach us: "*Oh Lord, our Lord, how excellent is Your name in all the earth!*" (Psalm 8:1a). David says, "*What is man that you should be mindful of him …*" (Psalm 8:4a). Before you get too far into your list of "things," get a glimpse of who God is and who you are. See His names as your palette. Let His glory colour your words and attitudes in prayer. This mindset will carry with you into the world. It must never be something you wear, but it should be seen.

> This pattern produces
> different prayer, and
> such prayer produces a
> different person.

Chapter 7
NAMES THAT COMMUNICATE

"… be Your name" (Matthew 6:9).

Why should God's name in particular captivate? The reason is simply that God's names are given to communicate who He is in language we can understand. They are names with very precise meanings and purpose. When we use them properly, we identify and acknowledge God's character in the name. This enables us to be intentional when we say it. God's names aren't mere tabs to facilitate conversation. His names declare who He is, and their use demands that we understand them, believe them, and are affected by the truths they express.

God Himself is the origin of the very concept of "Father." Not only is God the first of all fathers, but He has always been God the Father. He has no beginning and no end. His Son, the Lord Jesus, is the eternally begotten Son. The Spirit is the eternal Spirit. Such meditation in prayer, based upon the truth of the Word of God, will fill us with faith.

Our Father is not a novice father learning by His mistakes. He knows everything before it ever happens. He has also made provision for all events to come. He is the perfect Father, the standard every other father should strive to reflect.

Understanding God as Father will purge your heart of present-day cultural attitudes toward fathers. When we worship God for His fatherhood, we will be changed as fathers, and our expectation of fathers will change. It will be lifted to a higher level. Our respect for fathers will be enhanced. Perhaps our prayers for fathers will be more precise, more educated. Our prayers will certainly be improved, as we will be improved.

There is a relentless, even terrifying tone to the Bible verse that says "*the Lord will not hold him guiltless who takes His name in vain*" (Exodus 20:7b). Consider in our prayers the use of God's name as nervous punctuation. Perhaps we aren't good with words, or we feel a little awkward, but often we just thought that God didn't really care what we called Him! Learn the principles Jesus teaches us here. Be sure you're not careless in your use of God's name. This will affect the way you pray. It will please God, and it will also change you.

Chapter 8
Re-Setting Our Vision

If we follow the pattern, we're soon translated to a heavenly environment. Jesus guides us to consider the secret glories of our Father in heaven. He has given us a reason to delay our needs earlier when He told us "… *your Father knows the things you have need of before you ask Him*" (Matthew 6:8b). Your needs are being addressed as you worship. They may already have been addressed before you prayed.

Many of our needs are designed by the Lord to drive us to prayer. If you're praying, then that need may dissipate before you reach the next clause!

The first answer to prayer is the re-setting of our vision of God.

Our problems remain real, but in this heavenly environment, in the secret place of prayer, our Father declares His sovereignty by His name. He's in control, and nothing disturbs Him. We may still weep with human agony over real circumstances that may never change in this life. The contradiction of prayer is that despite the very real problems we face, another reality overrules. We find safety and security in the presence of God our Father.

Like a designer's pattern frees the tailor to personalize the detail in the actual garment, so this pattern frees the words from the ritual of repetition. It takes less than a minute to recite the Lord's Prayer, but to pray according to the pattern is limitless.

Ideally, prayer must avoid the confines of time. The present world silently enforces an unhelpful rush. Today it's difficult to find the quiet that prayer welcomes. Jesus counsels us to find the secret place of prayer. There to stop! There to stay! There to pray, "*Your kingdom come*" (Matthew 6:10).

Chapter 9
THE POINT TENSE

"Your kingdom come ... " (Matthew 6:10).

This is a startling request! We're asking for this world to come to an end! The Aramaic word "maranatha" gives us the sense of its use. It means "our Lord comes." It signifies a positive excitement about the world coming to an end. It's not a term of desperation, but it might indicate weariness. It's mostly the anticipation of glory. It's an exciting expectation. It was the prayer of the early church some two thousand years ago. Jesus places it right in the early parts of His pattern.

Once this request is answered, the rest of the Lord's Prayer will be redundant, as God's will is finally done on earth as it is in heaven. Hunger pangs will cease to pain the poor. There will be no more debt. We will have no debtors. There will be no more temptation. No more evil to fear. What a glorious day! No wonder the Church viewed this event with excitement. Lord, restore "maranatha" to your people again! Hear the creation groaning for release from the fall and its curse (Romans 8:22).

The final coming of God's Kingdom will be cataclysmic, but it's already coming in essence by the daily functioning of the Church in the world and in the lives of its members. A believing Church. A witnessing Church. A praying Church. A Church declaring God's Word to a needy world. A gospel-inspired church, all over the world crying out "Your Kingdom come!" A longing Church—watching, waiting, eager.

The word translated "come" in Matthew 6:10 is an interesting guide to our prayers for the Kingdom. Vine is helpful when he says: "Concerning the future, the Lord taught His disciples to pray, Thy Kingdom come, (Matt 6:10), where the verb (Come) is in the point tense, precluding the notion of a gradual progress and development, and implying a sudden catastrophe as declared in (2 Thess. 2:8)."[3] It is "*in a moment, in the twinkling of an eye, at the last trumpet*" (1 Corinthians 15:52a); "*He shall reign for ever and ever!*" (Revelation 11:15b).

---

[3] W.E. Vine, Merrill F. Unger, et al., s.v. "kingdom," *Vine's Complete Expository Dictionary of Old and New Testament Words* (Camden, NY: Thomas Nelson Publishers, 1985), 345.

Chapter 10
THE SOUND OF PRAYER

How should prayer for a cataclysmic event sound? What will its content be? Will it have energy? Will it sound like pathetic praying to the listener, or will it sound victorious? It may begin as either, but as we remind ourselves of God in prayer, surely prayer will become majestic and glorious in its expression! This is an awesome truth! The believer, in his secret, isolated room expects this cataclysmic event to happen any day now! In fact, it has been too many days already! We want Him now! Hear the church: "*How long, O Lord?*" (Psalm 13:1a).

Prayer may begin with pathos, but it should always end with power!

This emphasis given by Jesus shifts the concern of prayer from our problems to the ultimate solution promised in the eternal purposes of God—the coming Kingdom. Our daily ups and downs are thereby levelled out in priority and relevance and set into the context of eternity. A greater cause fills the believer's heart and mind. The Kingdom of God is coming. The Church must be engaged with the trials of life, in and out of itself, but the grand theme that determines the Church's character and personality in the world is the coming Kingdom. We are a victorious Church simply waiting—waiting for our King and His Kingdom to come.

This pattern of Jesus will rejuvenate our prayer meetings. Prayer will again become the life-blood of the individual and the church! This private anticipation will infect the general prayer meeting of the church with that same spirit. The local and universal church will return to being a church filled with energy. Could it be that we have lost this excitement in prayer?

Such an understanding of life and prayer will also produce the spontaneous outburst that is expressed in the next clause of the pattern: "*Your will be done …*"! (Matthew 6:10)

Chapter 11
GOD'S WILL FOR ME

"… Your will … " (Matthew 6:10).

God has a will, and this phrase is a call for the fulfillment of God's will. He has a purpose, an aim. God has a plan for the world, time, and eternity. Jesus invites us to take part in the fulfilling of God's will by praying for that fulfillment.

Our prayers are generally framed around our needs, our will. Of course, we then qualify this by saying "if it be your will." God's will isn't seen in Him deciding to fulfill our will. God's will is that we align with His will—which, of course, does involve me!

Many believers carry on in life with no concept of God's will. They only understand the idea of "His will for me." The first thing to grasp as you pray is this reality: God has a will! Jesus tells us that a primary purpose of prayer is the furtherance of God's will.

So pray for the fulfillment of His divine plan. God has thought it through and arranged it. He laid it out chronologically, geographically, and

God's will for me is to pray for God's will to be done.

theologically. He is fully invested in it. Above all else, He has determined the cost of it! It cost the giving of His only Son for me and you.

In this respect, God's will is about us in great measure, but the daily events of our life pale in the light of His divine plan. This phrase puts our salvation high in terms of priority, and the daily burdens of our life take on a more balanced weight, at times even becoming insignificant by comparison.

It was the will of God to give His Son for you. All through time, this plan was unfolding in the lives of people, as recorded for us in the Old Testament. Read about it in veiled form there. Then read the New Testament and see the plan unfold clearly. In the Gospels, Jesus was born of a virgin, lived a sinless life, and was declared innocent yet still condemned by the abdication of the greatest legal system in the world.

He was crucified at the demands of the greatest religion in the world. But God raised Him from the dead, and the risen Christ was seen by many witnesses. He gave instruction to His disciples to wait at Jerusalem, and the Holy Spirit descended upon them there. He came, and the Church was born. The Church from then till now has turned the world upside down.

We are the Church today. Jesus told us to pray that the will of God be done. God's will is bigger than my hospital appointment at this point in the pattern. It supersedes it in priority, because God intends to bring all our suffering to an end. But that's later. Right now it's still in preparation, and we're to pray for it. In praying for God's will to be done, we're praying that all of our sorrows and cares be laid to rest. God's will is the ultimate answer to all of our specific prayers. They are all subsumed under one single request: "Your will be done."

Notes

_____

_____

_____

_____

_____

Chapter 12
JESUS PRACTISED WHAT HE PREACHED

"… be done on earth …" (Matthew 6:10).

J esus illustrated this aspect of private prayer. See Him on earth, in the garden of Gethsemane, *"… take this cup away from Me; nevertheless not My will, but Yours, be done"* (Luke 22:42). This type of praying has spiritual grandeur and painful daily realities. In the garden, Jesus illustrates that there is an essential connection between prayer, God's will, and our sacrificial suffering here in this life.

This is certainly not about us earning our salvation or gaining merit. It is nevertheless about sacrifice. Jesus gave His life. God's will being done on earth involves us giving up our lives. This is the taking up of our cross daily spoken of by Jesus in Luke 9:23. When Jesus says to pray *"Your will be done on earth,"* He's bringing home to us the privilege of involvement in His suffering.

This pattern for prayer puts God in heaven, being worshipped as God and Father, with a will for what's done on the earth, thereby implying the Church's engagement in its outworking. Indeed, the individual praying believer will be partnering with God as they pray. What is prayer about today? It is fellowship with God in His will being done in the world. What a privilege! How we respond to trouble and difficulty exposes the reality of our engagement in God's will being done on the earth.

We must become familiar with God's plan for this world as it's laid out in the Bible. Read it and see in the Old Testament the declaration of the purposes of God in the world, in time. Read the New Testament and see all the prophecies fulfilled in Christ. Read the book of Acts and see the Church founded and engaged in turning the world upside down by preaching and sharing its message of free salvation in Christ. Read the New Testament letters and learn to walk with God in real daily terms. Then we certainly will pray informed, educated prayers.

God's will is not clockwork, set in motion and left to run. We are part of the active mechanism that brings it to pass, by our prayers and by our humble, willing obedience. I think when Jesus used these words to teach His disciples that day on the mount, He felt the pain of the Garden of Gethsemane. Jesus was practising what He preached.

As Jesus submitted to the will of God in the garden that day, Judas was busy working out his own will—and see the desperate outcome! When you pray too much about things you want God to do for you, think of that comparison.

Have we any detailed guidance on this grand enterprise? Yes! Jesus said it is to be done on earth "*as it is in heaven.*"

Chapter 13
BRINGING HEAVEN TO EARTH

"… as it is in heaven …" (Matthew 6:10)

God's will is fulfilled perfectly every moment in heaven, without hesitation, with absolute delight. There is no reluctance to obey in heaven, and there is anticipation and rejoicing at the fulfillment of God's will. That's what we must pray will happen here on earth. The present-day church wants the worship of heaven to come down to earth. Worship was addressed in the earlier phrase, "hallowed be your name." Here, God wants the obedience of heaven to be brought down to earth, so pray, "*Your will he done on earth … as it is in heaven.*"

This is a call, not a command. It represents the heart-cry of the believer. We are not capable of making God's will be done on the earth as it's done in heaven; however, it would be a highly desirable set of circumstances for the world. What a wonderful fulfilment His will is going to be for God and humanity.

Praying for the ideal raises our intentions to achieve it, privately in our own lives, then in the life of the Church, and finally out to the world by example. What effect does praying for others have on the one praying? When I personally pray for real change in others, does that have any effect on me? The answer is, without doubt, yes it does. It will influence you to better yourself. As you argue the case for improvement in your partner in prayer, detailing their failures and the need for improvement, it all comes back to strike your own heart, if you're genuine.

The old adage "point one finger at me, and you point three back at yourself" carries weight in prayer! We must understand what we're asking for. This is what the life of the Church is all about. We must learn how to take God's will to ourselves and show by example what it looks like on earth as it is in heaven. That is obedience with the character of heaven. It's cheerful, willing, energetic, and speedy cooperation to further God's will. Although this is not a command but a request, it does produce obedience in the life of the true believer and the believing church.

There is a point to using this part of the pattern. It benefits people everywhere, in the Church and outside of it, as believers love their enemies, preach the good news to the poor, and declare the message of God's free salvation in Christ. As they live lives that show the quality of God's family in their love for one another, they show what God's kingdom looks like.

It also has a sobering function at a different level. It means that the Church has brought heaven down to earth in the lives of its members. God can thereby reveal Himself to people through them. They should understand that a case is being raised against the world for its rejection of God's Kingdom. This rejection is expressed by their refusal to receive the message exampled in the life of the church. The verbal warnings of the gospel must be spoken clearly. To this end, the Church must be brave and speak with boldness and warn people that the Kingdom of God is coming.

Chapter 14
BETWEEN HEAVEN AND EARTH

The pattern now moves from heaven to earth. Before moving on, thinking about Hebrews 4:6 will help us to understand the purpose and benefit of prayer.

I have suggested that needs-based prayer is understandable but not a good standard. There is a better way to understand prayer. The writer to the Hebrews says, "*Let us therefore come boldly to the throne of grace, that we may obtain mercy and find grace to help in time of need*" (Hebrews 4:16). We often think that this verse is an invitation to ask for mercy and grace, for help in our time of need. However, the writer to the Hebrews says that we are to approach the throne of grace to *obtain* grace, mercy, and help in our time of need.

The word "obtain" certainly encompasses the meaning that we can ask and receive. But the Greek word translated here as "obtain" has a richer sense than merely asking and receiving. It also tells us that when we pray, we receive grace, mercy, and help … simply by being there in God's gracious presence by faith.[4]

---

[4] W.E. Vine, s.v. "obtain," *Vine's Complete Expository Dictionary of Old and New Testament Words* (Camden, NY: Thomas Nelson Publishers, 1985), 439.

No asking, pleading, or agony is required. We are approaching the throne of grace—that is, the free, unmerited favour of God. In this case, from the throne we freely receive grace, mercy, and help. Even those who feel no special need of God's intervention in their life will receive grace and mercy, simply by praying. When I use the word "praying," I refer to raising a matter according to the Lord's pattern, which we have been discussing in this book. If your prayer centres around desperate, heart-breaking needs, the misery you produce for yourself will outweigh the grace, mercy, and help that the Lord is trying to pour out upon you.

Is this not your experience? Surely God's presence provides us with mercy, grace, and help before we ever ask for it, either for ourselves or others. Asking is only one small part of the prayer, and as we shall see, it's quite far down the list of priorities suggested by Jesus.

How is this mercy, grace, and help given to us? We receive it because of the nature of God and the experience that awaits those who seek Him with all their heart. The pattern of prayer does nevertheless now turn to the theme of asking. What can we learn about this aspect of prayer?

Asking God for help is legitimate but must be controlled and kept subservient to worship and God's grand themes of redemption. When you need grace, mercy, or help in times of difficulty, follow Jesus's pattern for prayer. Long before the request is made, you will find that you've already received grace, mercy, and help from the Lord.

Let's now turn back to the text and the subject of the Lord's pattern. Here I will offer a gentle caution. I'm not suggesting that prayer can't contain requests, urgent or otherwise. However, it would be a healthy exercise to try praying for a week without making any requests at all.

The next clause we encounter contains the words "*give us.*" We'll look at the statement critically before sanctifying it, as Jesus does, by its context in the pattern.

Notes

_____

_____

_____

_____

_____

Chapter 15
THE FULCRUM

"Give us … " (Matthew 6:11)

Here we are at a fulcrum in the Lord's Pattern for prayer. So far, the pattern leads us upward to God in heaven, to His grand design for the world, time, and eternity. To His Fatherhood and divine character. To heaven itself, where God is. The Church's great anticipation is that His Kingdom comes. God's will is to be done on earth as it is in heaven!

Now we descend to meet ourselves in the rest of the pattern. We'll drop from the glory of God in heaven to the common needs, sins, and fears of people on earth.

From the glory of God to the troubles of men

The statement *"Give us"* is jarring, because the word "give" is often associated with avarice and greed. It can be a grasping, covetous entitlement. Isolated from the text, the word ironically calls to mind the proverb, *"The leech has two daughters—*(crying) *Give and Give!"* (Proverbs 30:15a). It's perhaps used here as a subtle caution to encourage us to listen to our own prayers and hear how often we use the language of "Give me!" It's a warning not to take your wants too far in prayer, and it reminds us that we've been given limited assurances of worldly comforts as followers of Jesus Christ. Nevertheless, we should ask for daily bread.

Despite all that I've just written, Jesus uses the word "give" in His pattern for us. It's not surprising that it's used here for that which is most wholesome, warm, pleasant, and comforting on a cold winter day—daily bread. In the pattern and its context, these words appear beautiful. There is no grasping, no greed. This is how to pray!

After properly preparing and approaching God, understanding and worshipping Him for who He is, and showing that our priority in prayer is to have God's will done above our own will, we're introduced to how to pray for our own needs. Our needs are summed up in these three words: "our daily bread." Let's look at them for guidance on the expansion of our prayers according to the pattern that warmly encourages us to pray: *"Give us this day…"*

Chapter 16
GOD SEES AND PROVIDES IN ADVANCE

"… this day … " (Matthew 6:11)

"This day" may be the demand of urgency or of desperation. In this context, it's often the honest need for communal efficiency. We can't function in prayer without bread daily. We're now in an altogether different type of praying. This is restrained, needs-based prayer.

It's a token of the Almighty's love for His children that long before we realize a need, He sees that need and makes provision for our daily bread. This should make breakfast for every believer a wonderful moment.

The Greek here could be translated "bread for the day" or "day by day." It's certainly not "bread for tomorrow." While the text may allow for this, Jesus's teaching on faith precludes it. He says *"Take therefore no thought for the morrow …"* (Matthew 6:34). The impression is given of a genuine recognition that we can't provide for ourselves, not even bread for this day.

As with every other phrase or clause in the pattern, these words should be thoughtfully expanded upon—like the master tailor carefully adjusting the pattern to fit the particular wearer, all while taking great care to maintain the original intention of the designer. Influenced by the pattern's divine choice of words, we can bring the phrase to bear on a world of needs. In many situations, we're not capable of meeting a need. God our Father loves to meet our needs, and He does so in a multitude of fascinating ways.

Take daily bread as an example of this divine providence. See a little brown seed being put into the ground in the spring of the year. For a time, nothing is visible. Then, imperceptibly pushing its way up through the earth, comes a tiny speck in a hundred acres of soil, a small green shoot. We can sum up the rest of the event to sunlight and rain and, eventually, a loaf of warm bread. This is a thorough example of the doctrine of God's providence. God plants provisions in advance of our needs in every department of life. They mature at exactly the right time, before life's winters. God planted the first seed in advance of humanity's need. Ever since Adam, despite the corruption of nature by the fall, people have had bread.

This may seem over simplified in the middle of a crises. Take note that these seeds were all created miraculously by God at the creation of the world. They have been maintained since then by His grace. We couldn't have created any of them. Science is parasitic. It can't create anything out of nothing. Take courage from this simple illustration of God's provision. Whatever your need, God can meet it this day simply because He has been preparing for it since before time began.

Chapter 17
THE "OUR" OF IDENTIFICATION

"... our ... " (Matthew 6:11)

This word "our" is not a claim to ownership. No, the bread is never ours! It must always be regarded as a gift from God. Yes, we planted it and farmed it, processed it and bought it back. But it was all a gift from a good God.

It's actually the "our" of identification, an acknowledgement of identification with the whole of humanity. Our common need of bread unites and divides us, and we often forget this obvious fact. People think they are gods, but every morning they wake up needing bread! This reminds us of the daily reality that defines us. Every day, each of us needs the good provisions of our God. The wisdom of prayer is that it helps us remember who we are while also addressing our needs. Who are we? We are permanent dependents. The word also reminds us that we're not dependent alone, not hungry alone. Every person is in daily need. It's *our* daily bread.

The principle of sharing blessings is contained in the word "our." Our needs are the same as other people's, and we should act on that. We should see ourselves as part of humanity, part of a family, part of a community, in particular if we're part of a church. Our own experience of need should turn our attention to those around us. The believer is generous because his Father, God, is generous.

Chapter 18
THE BASIC HUMAN NEED

"… daily bread" (Matthew 6:11)

Give us this day our *"daily bread."* It's the central clause in the pattern. The first section is about God; the second is about humanity. Bread is the bridge between them. Prayer is about everything, from the grand themes of divinity to the need for humble bread. A hungry king and the poor beggar will both be thankful for a piece of bread.

The devil tempted Jesus after forty days without His daily bread! He had been fasting that whole time and was hungry (Matthew 4:2). We're vulnerable to temptation when we have no bread. We're fertile ground for temptation when we're weak from hunger, and we may be tempted to steal bread or money for bread.

Hunger for anything is a dangerous place to be. Any human need for which we hunger brings a dark advantage for temptation. Stealing is not legitimate, even if we're hungry. Jesus tells us that prayer is the answer. The answer to every need begins in prayer.

When people fail to make plans for a famine, they blame God when they're hungry. It's legitimate to address God with your complaint if you were genuinely unable to prepare. But blaming God is always wrong. He may have allowed the problem to arise to teach us to pray. Remember that when you use this pattern!

The opposite is equally tempting and much more subtle. When we have too much bread, we stop relying on Him, vainly imagining we have no more need of His help. At the same time, we ignore our fellow humans who are still hungry and blaming God when they should be blaming us.

Pray that you might receive daily bread, or the basic essentials of life. Understand that when we pray "*Give us this day our daily bread*," we're asking that all of our temporal and spiritual needs be met—modestly.

Often when we're in need, the Lord Himself tries to get us back to a place of active trust in His wisdom and care. When we're given more than we need, the Lord enables us to help our brother, who may still be hungry. Daily bread is meant to indicate something sufficient for ourselves with some left over to share. The phrase is not intended to put us on a monastic diet.

All of heaven's resources will be engaged to bring us bread.

Note that this same God, our Father, will set in motion the power of divinity to release all the resources of heaven to bring us bread while we're still praying in our room…our *tameion*. (Greek for any private room and/or a "warehouse." See my first book, *THE ROOM*, chapters 10 and 11 for a full discussion on this point.)

Imagine all the power of God energized to work out His will in heaven and on earth. Consider the depth of insight, the energy of thought, the preparation, the resources. Consider the silent, divine influence of God's presence that causes His will to be done in heaven. On earth He can even make His enemies obey Him (Proverbs 16:7) . "*The king's heart is in the hand of the Lord …*" (Proverbs 21:1). Weigh all this creative power and authority. Weigh His omnipotence. See the power of His love at Calvary for us. Look at the power of the resurrection. All of this is set in motion to answer this diminutive cry: "*Give us this day our daily bread.*"

The request for bread is the first clear request for ourselves in Jesus's pattern of prayer. The next request is also for ourselves, but it's a different kind of necessity.

Notes

_____

_____

_____

_____

_____

Chapter 19
THE BASIC HUMAN PROBLEM

"And forgive us …" (Matthew 6:12)

Prayer begins by taking us to solitude in our own chamber. It then raises us to the throne of God in heaven and to His coming Kingdom. It brings us to the basic human need—daily bread. Then it takes us to the basic human problem—sin!

We often tumble into God's presence as though He had no standards for appearing before Him. Here is the standard: cleanliness! Unconfessed sin is a stain on a life. God is in heaven, and nothing that defiles shall enter there (Revelation 21:27). We need cleansing and forgiveness. We have seen reference to this in the early part of the pattern, but here, sin and the need for forgiveness are central.

In the NKJV, our sins are referred to as "*our debts*." Debt is a serious issue that has become all too common today. It has a deadening influence, like sin. Let's look at our debts.

Bread is the basic necessity for life. Forgiveness is the basic necessity for heaven.

The Greek word for "debt" is *aphiemi*, which means "to send forth, to send away … to remit and to forgive."[5] In Matthew 6:12, *aphiemi* means that debts will be completely cancelled, as will "sins."

In a section under the heading "Forgiveness," Vine tells us that it even "applies to the thoughts of our hearts ... Forgiveness signifies the remission of the punishment due to sinful conduct, the deliverance of the sinner from the (righteous imposed) penalty ... it involves the complete removal of the cause of the offence ... Such remission is based upon the vicarious and propitiatory work of Christ ... His substitutionary, atoning sacrifice."[6]

Jesus is referring to His soon-to-be-accomplished death and resurrection. Think about that! He hasn't been to the cross yet. At the Sermon on the Mount, the disciples didn't understand that the cross was coming, but Jesus knew!

Jesus gives us just a few words to deal with a lifetime of sin. As with the rest of the pattern, we can expand the base as much as we need. Never allow confession of sins to dominate your praying. It's a late arrival to the pattern. Forgiveness is where to dwell, and the purpose of forgiveness is to reset us on the path of service from the springboard of acceptance.

---

[5] W.E. Vine, Merrill F. Unger, et al., s.v. "aphiemi," *Vine's Complete Expository Dictionary of Old and New Testament Words* (Camden, NY: Thomas Nelson Publishers, 1985), 250.

[6] W.E. Vine, Merrill F. Unger, et al., s.v. "forgiveness," *Vine's Complete Expository Dictionary of Old and New Testament Words* (Camden, NY: Thomas Nelson Publishers, 1985), 250.

Chapter 20
A Helpful Concept

"… our debts … " (Matthew 6:12)

Jesus says three words: *"forgive us our debts."* We should never make light of our sins, but it would be a lie to think that you are the only sinner, or the worst, in the world or the Church. This plural principle in the Lord's Prayer makes the statement that "I am a sinner and so is everybody else." See this blunt statement in the New Testament: *"for all have sinned and fall short of the glory of God"* (Romans 3:23).

When I realize that I'm a sinner, it should be no comfort to read that everybody is sinful. Plurality here is meant to produce a sense of a universal humility: *"We have turned, everyone, to his own way"* (Isaiah 53:6b).

Our prayers are naive if this fundamental human condition is ignored while approaching a Holy God. Jesus encourages us to raise the issue of our moral and ethical debts, our sins. Debt is a helpful concept in grasping the nature of sin. It builds up, it gathers, it grows, it multiplies. It never goes away quietly on its own. It often requires urgent attention. The fact that someone else has more debt than I do does not alleviate my indebtedness!

When troubled by our own sins, we often feel that we will not be welcomed by God. Jesus's pattern invites anyone troubled by sin to come and pray, "forgive us our sins." The devil wants to extend our fall for as long as he can. He doesn't object to you confessing, as long as you stay steeped in your sense of failure a bit longer. He will wreck your day. Jesus knows that God is ready to forgive instantly and cleanse us, fill us, and give us a fresh start. God will make it a new day! Pray "*forgive us our debts*." Many believers feel unworthy at the Lord's Table, not realizing that it would be much worse if they thought they were worthy!

When you fall, pray "forgive us our" debts. Have you noticed that many of the sins we commit involve another person. When you ask for forgiveness, turn your mind to your brother, who is likewise struggling with sin. Pray that he will pick himself up and believe in the power of the gospel available to us all. Before long, you'll be rejoicing in the truths of the gospel you have just prayed for your brother and believe for yourself. The devil will leave you alone because he can't stay around truth or praise. Your brother may well be restored and forgiveness multiplied.

The sins we're to be initially concerned about are our own! When confronted by our own sins, we can experience an uncontrollable desire to escape. We've forgotten that Jesus tells us to pray "forgive us our sins." One of the purposes of prayer is to reset our relationship with God. He wants nothing to remain that disturbs our fellowship in prayer.

Every time we pray, we should confess our sins. We may be embarrassed by their frequency. God is not surprised yet always willing to forgive. When forgiveness is asked for and received, the work of Christ is exalted in heaven and on earth. Give Him glory, and come to Him for forgiveness often. Use embarrassment caused by your frequency as a lever to change. Keep your conscience clean. It will affect your daily life and maybe even affect your health.

Every time of prayer should reset our relationship with the Lord. It will also reset your moral day. Settling accounts sets your day on a foundation of peace. Prayer may find us heavy of heart due to many things, but it can change us when we follow this pattern and not just recite it as a bland religious rite. Not the dead letter, but a living word spoken by Jesus Himself. Surely this will enliven the solitary, weary believer. Pray "*forgive us our debts.*" But there is a condition!

This isn't the kind of condition that balances weight in a business deal. This condition simply reveals our heart as genuine, because "*the hope of the hypocrite shall perish*" (Job 8:13b).

Notes

_____

_____

_____

_____

_____

Chapter 21
FORGIVEN AND FORGIVING

"… as we forgive our debtors … " (Matthew 6:12)

Regarding Matthew 6:12, Vine says, "Human forgiveness is to be strictly analogous to divine forgiveness." To substantiate his case, he quotes Matthew 6:12 and says, "There is no limit to Christ's' forgiveness."[7]

If we don't forgive our debtors, we will conversely but justly come to doubt God's forgiveness of our debts. We'll stumble through our Christian life with doubts and insecurity about God's love for us, and we'll lose our peace and joy, all because we refuse to forgive others. If you want to be confident about God's forgiveness, first forgive those who sin against you!

Willingness to forgive will bring the blessing of God. But it may not necessarily remove the pain caused by the offence. Consequences can be very troubling.

The forgiven man is a forgiving man.

What is the Bible's rationale for healing such unjust pain? To answer that question, let's go to the cross. There Jesus was

---

[7] Ibid.

unjustly judged by a Roman court and condemned to death by the greatest religion the world has ever known. This travesty of justice was then enacted by Roman soldiers, who beat him mercilessly for pleasure. Then with all the cruel, crude precision of the warrior, they confirmed His death with a spear—but not before Jesus spoke some of His last words on the cross.

Jesus prayed on the cross, "*Father, forgive them; for they know not what they do*" (Luke 23:34, KJV). Consider your response, your attitude, toward your enemy. As convincing evidence of our forgiveness for our enemies, God wants to hear us pray for blessings to be poured out upon them. This kind of prayer shows that we have forgiven our debtors. Peace is the evidence of a forgiving heart. This radical love makes believers stand out from their fellow sinners, but more, it declares our God to be glorious.

Don't be that man in James who looked into a mirror and forgot (James 1:24). The pattern will make prayer memorable. Aim to make forgiveness end a matter. The aim is peace. Real peace. Peace with God and people.

If you deal with forgiveness properly, you'll find the place of prayer to be a place of joy and ease. If your prayer times are unsubstantial, despite all your preparation of place, consider this clause in the Lord's pattern.

Jesus sees forgiveness as crucial for effective prayer, or He wouldn't have put it into the pattern. Never rush confession and forgiveness. They are life's resets. They bring us back to a good place—the cross. That's a good starting point for a day and an essential end to every day.

However, consciousness of sin must never become what we are about or who we are. We are Christ's redeemed, forgiven children. Salvation in Christ today must carry the message of *"good tidings of great joy"* (Luke 2:10). If the Christian dwells too much on sinful failure, how will he or she experience joy? Those who do proceed, at Christ's invitation, to go through the narrow gate will eventually give up and sit down at the edge of the King's Highway in despair. The gospel is not about having a miserable life due to our failures. It's a humble life due to God's prevailing grace, mercy, and peace—despite our failings!

So actively rejoice in forgiveness received. Take joy in forgiving others, and continue in this pattern of prayer as it deals with our daily Christian walk in this world that's filled with temptation. And so …

Notes

_____

_____

_____

_____

_____

Chapter 22
FINDING WHERE YOUR HEART IS

"And do not lead us … " (Matthew 6:13)

The request to not be led must be understood as an expression of a spontaneous revulsion of sin. It is evidence of the Christ within us.

In the garden, Jesus prayed, "… *take this cup away from Me; nevertheless not My will, but Yours, be done*" (Luke 22:42). This is in part about the physical pain of the cross, but much more, Jesus is recoiling at the thought of taking sin upon Himself. In whatever light we understand this, the identification with sin repulses the holy Son of God. Paul wrote, "*For He made Him who knew no sin to be sin for us*" (2 Corinthians 5:21a). Believers share this revulsion in increasing measure as they pray according to the pattern. As we pray, our understanding of temptation, both practical and theological, expands.

Temptation itself is not sin. Jesus was "… *in all points tempted as we are, yet without sin*" (Hebrews 4:15b). Temptation often comes as a test to show us where our heart is. Testing is necessary and healthy but nonetheless unsettling. So we ask the Lord not to lead us there.

This part of the pattern is also intended to keep us vigilant, to remind us of our weaknesses, and to remind us that we're in a battle and must succeed. We are being strengthened by victory and humbled by failure. Both contribute to real spiritual growth if handled properly.

We constantly think of failure in conjunction with the word "temptation"; however, we are enabled to resist temptation by the means of grace, as found in the life of the Church and our own private devotions, especially the reading of God's Word and prayer.

Chapter 23
NOT NEGATIVE … NECESSARY

"… into temptation …" (Matthew 6:13)

Our homes and churches should be places where temptation is actively kept to a minimum. We control these spaces, and they should actively feed our souls and protect us and our children from temptation.

We are told to pray *"lead us not into temptation."* Our battle against sin is a fundamental part of the believer's existence. The believer's life, in part, is about putting off sin and embracing godliness.

The praying sinner is building a relationship with a holy God. Part of sanctification is the command to be holy because God is holy. Preparation for heaven is called sanctification, and it involves growing in grace and the knowledge of Jesus. It's also about living right, forsaking sin, refusing temptation, and putting on Jesus Christ.

Many people think prayer is about receiving comfort in trouble and help when we're weak. Yes, but it's also about keeping us from sin. If we aren't conscious of the battle of temptation, then we're not walking with God, because that battle is a daily part of our walk with Him.

Bible scholars have studied this verse. The Greek word for "temptation" is *peirazo*, which means to "Assay … to try, to test, to prove." It's also used to denote the testing of a piece of metal to determine its quality, ingredients, and concentration.[8]

The idea is not to destroy something or someone. It's not even necessarily connected to temptation to sin as such. Jesus was tempted and is "… *able to aid those who are tempted*" (Hebrews 2:18b). Even our victory over temptation may improve us and strengthen us to support others.

May God prove that we are the real thing. Temptation can expose weaknesses we didn't realize were there. Resisting temptation strengthens us. Hebrews 2:18 is positive in its tone. The idea of testing is not negative. Failing is. There must be the possibility of failure when we're tested, otherwise we'd never understand our limits. God tests us to prepare us, to help us help others. Never fall into the trap of imagining that every temptation ends in sin! Jesus was in all points tempted yet without sin. He instructs us to pray "*And lead us not into temptation, but deliver us from evil*" (Matthew 6:13a. KJV).

---

[8] Della Thompson (Ed.,), s.v. "assay," *The Oxford Compact English Dictionary* (Oxford, UK: Oxford Press, 1996), 53.

Chapter 24
The Final Deliverance

"... deliver us from evil ... " (Matthew 6:13, KJV)

This final clause of the pattern is the daily desire of godly society. Prayer that follows Jesus's pattern produces a hunger to see the end of this evil age and the return of Christ to take us to Himself. This prayer is a request for the final end of evil. It focuses more on our final deliverance than on skirmishes. It's not so much about daily events but a final end to all evil.

Evil here is both general and specific. Evil comes in many different guises and can be present in all aspects of life. It therefore is the perfect word with which to end this pattern. It allows us to pray for everything that adversely affects us, but it's placed at the end of the pattern. This should help us to keep it in check and not to give it more prayer time than necessary.

Prayer is about our Father God; it's about His purposes, His will being done. It's about our need for bread, forgiveness, and being kept in and from temptation. It reminds us to forgive if we would be forgiven. Evil is placed at the end of the prayer to limit its expression, lest the subject of evil supplant the worship of God or our own daily needs. Also, it's last because it sums up the entire prayer. When the Kingdom of God comes in its fullness at the return of Christ, we will be delivered from evil in all its expressions.

The clause "*deliver us from evil*" is a significant aid to self-examination. If we don't find this desire for deliverance burning in us after prayer, then perhaps prayer that day was sleepy, or worse. We should check our prayers at every clause. At every point our heart is revealed by its response to the issue raised by the pattern.

Believers address God as Father with a sense of wonder! There is excitement when we think of Heaven. Believers yearn for His kingdom to come. We long to see the demise of temptation and evil. Believers feel the need of forgiveness. Praying believers heartily forgive. Our response to the pattern reveals our heart.

This last clause should produce in every believer a rush of prayer. Not a dreary end wishing for rest in heaven, but a heightened anticipation of His coming in victory. The glorious return of Jesus Christ, King of kings and Lord of lords. Maranatha…Lord, come quickly!

The End

Thank you for reading my humble book. If you've benefitted from this book, or have any questions, please send me an email. I would love to chat with you.

Archie Murray
Southern Ontario
Canada
archiemurray7@gmail.com

Notes

_____

_____

_____

_____

_____

OTHER BOOKS BY ARCHIE MURRAY

There are three books in this series so far. Although they are stand-alone books, they do form one discussion on prayer. The series adheres to the natural flow of Jesus's teaching on prayer found in the Sermon on the Mount.

The Room: Preparation for Prayer
The Room serves as a prologue to the Lord's Prayer. Often we forget to prepare and instead rush in where angels fear to tread. Jesus tells us to go into our room!

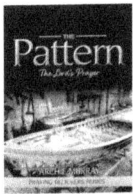

The Pattern: The Lord's Prayer
The Pattern is the actual text of The Lord's Prayer, which is the most used, most abused, and most ignored prayer in the Bible. In this book, the prayer is explained and expanded upon.

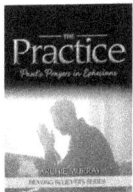

The Practice: Paul's Prayers in Ephesians
The Practice provides an example of real prayer as found in Paul's prayers in Ephesians. There Paul tells his readers what he actually prays for when praying for them.

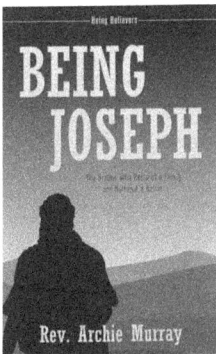

Being Joseph (978-1-4866-1573-5)
Have you ever felt betrayed by a family member? Have you ever needed even a glimpse of hope to help you through a tough situation? In the Old Testament, we read that Joseph was thrown into a pit and then sold by his own brothers. This great betrayal left him feeling alone and in despair. Unfortunately, this was only the beginning of his troubles.

Being Joseph takes a closer, pastoral perspective on perseverance through hardships, the value of forgiveness even when it's near impossible, and the redemptive hope of reconciliation. Joseph's story expands on dreams, slavery, seduction, imprisonment, and the restoration of a family. In the worst moments of Joseph's life, we can see that God never left his side. The lessons we can learn from this book can help enrich our daily lives in this difficult world today.

All ages will benefit from this captivating commentary on a real family, just like yours.

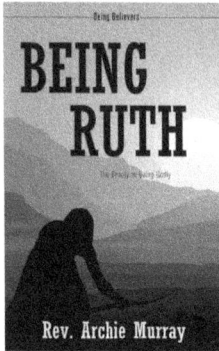

Being Ruth (978-1-4866-1709-8)

Have you ever felt like your faith was being tested? Have you ever experienced the death of a loved one? The book of Ruth, found in the Old Testament, is a moving story of a sad tragedy followed by an unrelenting commitment, both human and divine. Ruth's sadness is followed by hope deferred, yet undeterred.

Being Ruth takes a closer pastoral perspective on the shape of human expressions and relationships, the significance of names, and the consequences of men dying childless. We see Ruth, the committed daughter-in-law to Naomi, responding with grace during a difficult time in life. Although this is not your typical love story, as you allow the Scriptures to speak you'll find a beautifully enchanting story.

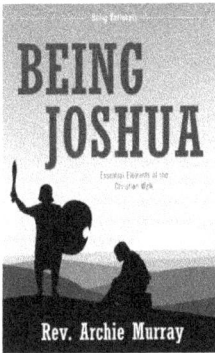

Being Joshua (978-1-4866-2213-9)

Have you ever wanted to be stronger, more vibrant, as a believer? Have you ever felt the church is weak when it should be strong? Have you ever felt that rampant evil should be shut down? Do you believe change is possible in the world, in the church… in you?! Joshua experienced a bad start in life—forty years in slavery. He wandered a desert for another forty years. Yet it was in and from these experiences that he discovered the believer's strength. He escaped slavery and went on to shut evil down and conquer the Promised Land. If we want to conquer the world for God… we must allow God first to conquer us.

Being Joshua shows how God uses the circumstances of life to change us into who He wants us to be. In life's slavery and wanderings, Joshua teaches us how to synapse with God's Spirit. Joshua teaches us that God is doing something—we are a part of it, but it is bigger than us. Joshua teaches us how to view life within the purposes of God and gain victory over our circumstances and ultimately ourselves. Joshua shows us that the weakest and the strongest believers need to encourage themselves and be strong. He reminds us, pertinent to our times, that we must also encourage each other. Joshua learned this from the Old Testament Scriptures taught in a godly family life, a community of believers, and a personal walk of faith in God. His education was by words and examples in real daily life. This book is written from a pastoral and practical perspective.

Watch for the next book in the
Praying Believers Series: The Practice!